25 Years,
25 Lessons

25 Years, 25 Lessons

LETTERS TO A BRIDE FROM A SEASONED WIFE

CHRIS BAXTER

Published by MC Publishing
www.respitefortheweary.com

Scripture quotations taken from the New American Standard Bible®,
Copyright © 1960, 1962, 1963, 1968, 1971, 1972, 1973, 1975, 1977, 1995
by The Lockman Foundation. Used by permission. (www.Lockman.org)

ISBN: 9780692981689
Editors: Dayna Moseley and Madelaine Singleton
Graphic Design: Roy Roper (roy@wideyedesign.net)
Illustrations: ©Adobe Stock

Printed by IngramSpark Print-On-Demand Services.

To Molly,
and all the brides you represent...

Thank you, Mother,
for teaching me sacrificial love...

Thank you, Mev,
my mother-in-law, for showing me always a gentle and quiet spirit...

Thank you, Mac,
my husband, for choosing me. I am delighted to be your wife.

Written in His love,
Chris

To The Reader

In 2005, my husband and I celebrated our fifteenth wedding anniversary. That same year, my sweet younger cousin-in-law, Molly Rutherford, became engaged. The Lord used both of these factors to put me in a reflective state of mind concerning marriage.

What have I learned during these years of my life?

What does God want me to keep learning and applying?

What words of wisdom could I give to a young married woman?

I began to answer each of these questions in the form of letters written to Molly. The fifteen letters are written to her, but really, for all to read and glean from.

And then, ten years of life went by; Molly and Ryan celebrated 10 years of marriage (which brought them four children), and Mac and I celebrated our twenty-fifth anniversary (which brought us an empty-nest from our four children). This particular anniversary was yet another reflective time; therefore, ten more letters were written. These ten learned-lessons pertain to this particular stage of married life.

I share all of these letters with you from a humbled position, knowing full well that I am still, even now, in the learning process as I walk the road of life with my husband. Many days are great; there's compatibility, laughter, and contentment. But honestly, some days are just the opposite; we miss each other's thoughts and intentions, and it's just plain hard. But it's in these hard places that rich and long-lasting lessons are learned. I pray these 25 years' worth of lessons that have been engrained in me through life experience, will be helpful to you not only as a newlywed, but also for many years to come.

Table of Contents

The Foundational Letter:
The High Gift of Marriage......2

1. The Love of Your Life,
   the Love of Your Soul.........6

2. Put on Love 10

3. On Submissiveness 14

4. The Gentle and Quiet Spirit.....18

5. Prayer is Powerful. 22

6. Fill His Needs 26

7. Be an Encourager 30

8. On Resolving Conflict 34

9. On Forgiveness. 38

10. Laugh Often. 42

11. Wife, Mother, Other 46

12. A Healthy Hobby 50

13. Together Time 54

14. Daddy, the Hero. 58

15. Keep Growing 62

10 YEARS LATER,
10 MORE LESSONS

16. Backwards, Forwards,
    and a Lot in Between 68

17. Interesting Order 72

18. Extended Love 76

19. Remember, He's a Man 80

20. Wise Counsel 84

21. Soften the Stiff Neck 88

22. Love in the Making 92

23. Who He Is, Not Who He Isn't . . .96

24. Decide Today, about Tomorrow . .100

25. Something New 104

Foundational Letter

You will also be a crown of beauty in the hand of
the Lord, and a royal diadem in the hand of
your God. It will no longer be said to you, "Forsaken,"
nor to your land will it any longer be said, "Desolate";
But you will be called "My delight is in her," and
your land "Married"; For the Lord delights in you …

Isaiah 62:3-4

The High Gift of Marriage

The kingdom of heaven is like a merchant seeking
fine pearls, and upon finding one pearl of great value,
he went and sold all that he had, and bought it.

Matthew 13:45-46

The High Gift of Marriage

Dear Molly,

This letter was not written first, but it will come first, because it's foundational to all the others. I just got back from your wedding, and I learned yet another lesson in marriage. I have been taught this before, but now I want to treasure this truth: marriage is a high gift from heaven. Husband and wife have the awesome privilege of portraying the beautiful picture of God's love for his people.

- On your wedding day, I witnessed Ryan's intense and intentional adoration for you; similarly, Christ, the Groom, pursues His cherished bride with steadfast love.

- You are Ryan's one pearl of great value; likewise, we are the Lord's prized possession.

- I imagine Ryan's heart was pounding with great expectation as you walked down the aisle towards him; in the same way, God's heart rejoices when His people answer His beckoning plea of, "Come".

- Molly, your love for Ryan radiated through your beauty. Your smile and your eyes said, "I am yours"; likewise, God's people are made complete when their hearts are turned to Him.

- Also, your wedding was worshipful; the bridesmaids, family, and friends were full of joy. Similarly, the angels in heaven celebrate when one sinner says, "I do."

- And finally, the preparation for your wedding was thought through explicitly and uniquely – the flowers, your dress, the music. This is a mere picture of us as the bride, when we will someday stand before our Husband in unblemished white at the final wedding feast.

Thank you, Molly, for this refresher lesson concerning the intense love between the bride and groom, between God and His people. I pray you will cherish this high gift of marriage for years to come.

Love, Chris

And I saw the holy city, new Jerusalem,
coming down out of heaven from God,
made ready as a bride adorned for her husband.

REVELATION 21:2

The Lord appeared to him from afar,

saying "I have loved you with an everlasting love;

therefore I have drawn you with loving-kindness."

Jeremiah 31:3

The Love of Your Life, The Love of Your Soul

And as the bridegroom rejoices over the bride,

so your God will rejoice over you.

Isaiah 62:5

The Love of Your Life, The Love of Your Soul

Dear Molly,

I, like you, had the privilege of marrying the **love of my life.**

I am so thankful to be married to my "knight-in-shining armor." In the very early stages of "wedded bliss," I learned my first lesson concerning marriage. After only a few months, I became very aware of the fact that my "knight" was human. He got tired; he made mistakes; sometimes, he failed me completely. I became confused and disappointed because I thought he was to be the one to "fill my cup." I expected him to meet my every need. Where had the in-love feeling of the anticipating engagement gone? The happily-ever-after had been invaded too quickly by the reality of life. Mac's love letters were replaced with the hard, exhausting work of a medical resident. I was in a new city, away from all family. As a newlywed, life with my man was hard, and I was lonely.

I, like you, have the privilege of knowing the **Love of my soul.**

God used this time, however, to draw me closer to Him and His perfect love. Learning of His deep love for my soul has been the basis of everything else God has taught me concerning life and marriage. In His Word, and over time and maturity, He has clearly shown me

His unfailing love. I both know and believe … *He calls me by name … He draws me with loving-kindness … He rejoices over me with shouting … He always sees me as a bride … He is the One who fills my cup, my every need (Isaiah 43:2; Jeremiah 31:3; Zephania 3:17; Isaiah 62:5; Psalm 16:5).* God's love for me does not fail. Knowing Jesus' love for my soul allows me to let go of the unattainable expectations I humanly tend to place on my husband. When these expectations have been lifted off my husband's shoulders, I then can enjoy him, and he enjoys me.

I encourage you to seek and continually find the great mystery of life, Jesus. His love for you is incredible, intentional, and infallible. Your husband's love for you is a sweet reflection of this love. I pray Christ's unfailing love will be the perfect bond of unity that ties your marriage together. Because then, you will live joyfully ever after, no matter the circumstances.

Love, Chris

"And I will betroth you to Me forever;
yes, I will betroth you to Me in righteousness and in justice,
in loving-kindness and in compassion,
and I will betroth you to Me in faithfulness. Then you will know the Lord."

HOSEA 2:19-20

Put on Love

Put on the new self ... Christ is all, and in all ...
put on a heart of compassion, kindness, humility,
gentleness, and patience; bearing with one another,
and forgiving each other ... and beyond all these things
put on love, which is the perfect bond of unity.

Colossians 3:10-14

Put on Love

Dear Molly,

This is God's plan for your marriage: stay rooted and grounded in the love of Christ. Remember, God's love is the *perfect bond of unity*. Daily seek Him, so you can then daily love your husband.

I want to recommend a book called **The Five Love Languages** by Gary Chapman. This particular book has been a wonderful asset to me in understanding how I can best daily love my husband. The five languages described in the book are: physical touch, acts of service, gift-giving, words of affirmation, and quality time. Showing all these languages is essential in your marriage, but realize some are more prominent in speaking love to your particular man. Knowing his love languages will help you direct your energy and focus. For example, in our marriage, Mac appreciates a home-cooked meal (drats), which is an act of service. But of course, I appreciate a date with him alone, which is quality time. So, we have learned to give to each other – I work in the kitchen; he takes me out. (Bless him.) Also, words of affirmation are important to both of us. I have realized I need to be intentional in building him up as a husband, as a daddy, and as a doctor. And he has realized well-thought through, uplifting words are like a bouquet of flowers for me. Find out each other's love languages and speak them intentionally.

Realize this too, sometimes loving is easy and sometimes it's not. That's why Scripture says to put on love. We, because of sin, are not able to love others more than we love ourselves. But if we *take off the old self… and put on the new (Ephesians 4:22-24)*, which is Christ in us, we can love in this self-sacrificing way. For example, sometimes making a home-cooked meal after a long stressful day is the absolute last thing I want to do. But for the sake of family unity, I want to provide dinners at home for Mac and the children a reasonable amount of nights each week. Thankfully, Mac is not overly picky concerning the food set before him. (Bless him again!) For you, there may be another entirely different way to speak love to your husband. Ask the Lord to show you what that is, and then decide to do it.

I encourage you to call on Christ in time of need. His strength will help you love your husband in spite of your up and down emotions, your potentially ongoing fatigue, or your differing stressful circumstances. These things are the reality of life, so don't wait for the "perfect peaceful time" to love. *Christ is all, and in all* no matter your reality… and through His strength, you can *put on love.*

Love, Chris

But put on the Lord Jesus Christ.

ROMANS 13:14

On Submissiveness

Wives, be subject to your own husbands,
as to the Lord. For the husband is the head
of the wife, as Christ also is the head of the church,
He himself being the Savior of the body.
But as the church is subject to Christ,
so also the wives ought to be to their husbands
in everything. Husbands, love your wives,
just as Christ also loved the church
and gave Himself up for her ...

Ephesians 5:22-25

On Submissiveness

Dear Molly,

The second I hear the phrase *be submissive* is the very second I want to rebel! Why is respect of authority so important to the Lord? The answer: because He knows that having and maintaining a submissive spirit is the woman's key to her husband's heart.

We are given a beautiful example of how this relationship works when looking at Christ and His bride, the church. When we as believers completely entrust our lives and lay down our control, Christ then is able to fully love and to fully lead. We cannot receive His love or His leadership without submitting to His Spirit. This picture is meant to speak into your marriage. As you submit to your husband's authority, he is able to love you and to lead you more freely. In so doing, your identity is not lost; quite the opposite, it's enhanced. As I respect my man and as a result, receive his love, I then become a much stronger, confident woman. So, do not look at this position as an awful curse when God meant it to be a bountiful blessing in your life. Your submission opens the door to your husband's desire to give you his self-sacrificing love. I have done it both ways, taking stubborn control and choosing to respect; each time, I have found out that only one Way really works for my best interest.

I want to also encourage you to not base your calling of submissiveness on whether or not your husband is fulfilling his calling of love and leadership to your expected standards. That's called conditional love. I challenge you to continually obey and pray. Obey the Lord – continue to submit in spite of the lack of love or the lack of leadership on your husband's part. Do not take the reins in your marriage; it will only contribute to passivity. But also, you must pray. Pray continually to the Lord to convict and teach your husband to do his part. He's a work in progress, just like you.

So remember, as you submit, you are giving your husband honor and respect – two qualities that compel your husband's heart to love and to cherish you. You, then, will become his prized possession that he desires to both pour into and protect. You will also find he wants to honor your requests, your ideas, and your wisdom. As a result, husband and wife are fulfilling their God given roles, and your marriage becomes a beautiful picture for all to see.

Love, Chris

Wives, be submissive to your own husbands
so that even if any of them are disobedient to the word,
they may be won without a word by the behavior of their wives,
as they observe your chaste and respectful behavior.

1 PETER 3:1-2

*And let not your adornment be merely external ...
but let it be the hidden person of the heart, with
the imperishable quality of a gentle and quiet spirit,
which is precious in the sight of God.*

1 Peter 3:3-4

The Gentle and Quiet Spirit

*Abide in Me, and I in you. As a branch cannot
bear fruit of itself, unless it abides in the vine,
so neither can you, unless you abide in Me.*

John 15:4

4

The Gentle and Quiet Spirit

Dear Molly,

I truly believe one of the greatest assets in a marriage relationship is when the wife obtains the *imperishable quality of a gentle and quiet spirit.* If it is *precious in the sight of God*, you know it will also be precious to your husband as well.

How can we, as wives, gain and keep this peaceful virtue? Notice 1 Peter 3 says the gentle and quiet spirit is born from the *hidden person of the heart;* and there is only one Person who can develop your innermost being. Jesus *is* the gentle and quiet Spirit! Decide to sit close by your Savior every morning. Let the Author of peace breathe into you through His Word. He will bring solitude to your heart in this chaotic world.

Realize this quiet disposition does not imply weakness in your wifely position or your God-given personality. On the contrary, *His gentleness will make you great (Psalm 18:35).* To illustrate, think of the beauty and purity of velvety rose petals. In order for these petals to even blossom, they must first be supported by a strong, life-sustaining stem. Likewise, the tenacious qualities of strength and wisdom stand underneath the beautiful attributes of contentment and peace. When you are rooted and grounded in the love of Christ, you will find out that nothing can shake your stable character or your calm reserve. At the very same time, your sweet fragrance of gentleness is an attraction to all.

I encourage you to be quiet enough in your spirit to hear the voice of the Lord, so when you relate to your husband, you will know when to speak and when to remain silent, when to confront and when to let something go. Trust the Lord to speak to you, and then, through you. Understand this too, sometimes the less you say, the more God is able to speak. Your words may touch your husband's ears, but God's words will penetrate his heart. Trust Him to speak clearly and concisely to your man, and let your gentle and quiet spirit *win him without a word (1 Peter 3:1)*.

Love, Chris

The fruit of the Spirit is…gentleness.
The fruit of the Spirit is … peace.
GALATIANS 5:22-23

In quietness and trust is your strength.
ISAIAH 30:15

Prayer is Powerful

Be anxious for nothing, but in everything
by prayer and supplication with thanksgiving
let your requests be made known to God.
And the peace of God, which surpasses all comprehension,
shall guard your hearts and your minds in Christ Jesus.

Philippians 4:6-7

5

Prayer is Powerful

Dear Molly,

Pray, pray, pray. I'll say it again, morning, noon, and night, pray, pray, pray. Your faith-filled words touch the heart of God and ignite His power! Put prayer into practice very early in your marriage so you may begin to reap the benefits with joy. As you present your requests to God concerning your husband, the Creator of his heart willingly moves and molds his character.

Prayer also enables you to maintain the gentle and quiet spirit (mentioned in the previous letter). Instead of pointing out all of your husband's flaws with a judgmental spirit toward him, quietly take these issues to the One who can groom and grow him into a mighty man of God. This approach will keep you from nagging him, which only causes your husband to turn away, not towards you. (Believe me, I am still learning – nagging doesn't get me anywhere.) But always believe and know this: God's power can change a man's heart and mind long before a wife's contentious words. Again, take these requests to the One who is able to make impossible things possible!

Here are some ways I have prayed for my husband over these many years.

I pray for him…

1. to have a deep love for God, His word, and for others

2. to understand me – my thoughts, my personality, my fears, my dreams

3. to be the spiritual leader of this family as a husband and a father

4. to surround himself with godly friends who will encourage him and keep him accountable to God's word and ways.

Over time, I have seen God at work in the heart of my husband. I love how He works (when I get out of the way)! He is for me; He is for my husband; and He is for our marriage. The same is true for you. Take advantage of the awesome privilege of prayer, and watch God work powerfully in your husband's life, and in your marriage.

Love, Chris

....the prayer of the upright is His delight.

PROVERBS 15:8

The (husband's) heart is like channels of water in the hand of the Lord;
He turns it wherever He wishes.

PROVERBS 21:1

Fill His Needs

Then the Lord God said,

"It is not good for man to be alone;

I will make him a helper suitable for him."

Genesis 2:18

6 Fill His Needs

Dear Molly,

When you said the simple words "I do" before God and man on your wedding day, you were committing yourself to the life-long privilege of being a helpmate to your husband. Realize this is now the first and foremost call in your life. This is God's will for you; and you, Molly, are the one suitable for Ryan. In obedience to God, decide to help your husband. Here are three broad ways we, as wives, are called to fill our husband's needs:

Physically. I encourage you to go to Song of Solomon in Scripture and see the intimate relationship between husband and wife. Remember, this is a need of your husband. Fill it – often.

Emotionally. Please know and always remember your husband needs you to be his confidant, his "safe place." Be quiet-spirited and listen to him. Then show kindness towards him – kind words, kind ways. Being kind in your thoughts and actions concerning your husband will keep a sweet peace within the walls of your home. Make it your ambition to encourage (put courage in) him every day. *Pleasant words are as honeycomb, sweet to the soul and healing to the bones (Proverbs 16:24)*.

Spiritually. Your husband needs you to grow spiritually. You are now *one flesh (Genesis 2:24)*, so when you grow, he grows. As you gain wisdom and knowledge concerning the love of Christ, you are able to speak into your husband's heart and mind with words of life. Realize a woman has the amazing ability to persuade a man, for better or for worse. Look at Scripture – Eve with Adam, Delilah with Samson, Sarah with Abraham, and more. I encourage you to speak into Ryan's days wisely and selflessly. Seek God's will first, and then speak into your husband's life. In doing so, you will both receive a blessing from the hand of the Lord.

Ryan needs you, Molly – physically, emotionally, and spiritually. You have been given the high honor of helping your husband be all he was created to be.

Love, Chris

The heart of her husband trusts in her,
and he will have no lack of gain.
She does him good and not evil all the days of her life.

PROVERBS 31:11-12

An excellent wife is the crown of her husband.

PROVERBS 12:4

An excellent wife, who can find?

For her worth is far above jewels.

Proverbs 31:10

Be an Encourager

A soothing tongue is a tree of life,

but perversion in it crushes the spirit.

Proverbs 15:4

Be an Encourager

Dear Molly,

Years ago, when I was standing with Mac at our wedding ceremony, my pastor was directing words towards me concerning my role as a wife. He encouraged me to take the position as "cheerleader" for my husband. He said I would become the "heartbeat of the home," both as a wife and then as a mother. Now, fifteen years and four children later, I have to say he was right. My disposition does affect the entire household. In this regard, I must choose daily, through Christ, to put my temporal, ever-swaying moods aside (God help me!) and "cheer" for my husband and family. The heartbeat of my words should be uplifting and directed, not deflating and misguided. My job, and yours, is to be our husband's encourager each and every day in the home, so he may be adequately equipped when he walks out of the home.

My first piece of advice in this area of encouragement is to listen. There will be many times your man will come home exhausted and possibly defeated from a hard day's work. Give him a safe place to escape the worries and stresses of this world. Hear him; pray for him. *The heart of her husband trusts in her, and he will have no lack of gain (Proverbs 31:11).*

Secondly, speak. Use choice words. Always be ready to build into his character. Be consciously aware that the words you choose to say have a direct impact on the man he will become. Your words can bring courage or cowardice into his heart. Be on his team; be his cheerleader. *A man (your husband) has joy in an apt answer, and how delightful is a timely word (Proverbs 15:23).*

A third thought: **never shame** your husband. Nothing positive will come from this negative route. Remember, God brought you to your particular man in order to help him, not hurt him. Hold his hand; lift him up. He does have weaknesses and he will make mistakes simply because he's human. But your responsibility is to bring his character, strengths *and* weaknesses before the Lord. God always desires to use weakness as an opportunity to display His strength. Allow Him to work; do not crush your husband's spirit while God is trying to mold it. God's purpose is to make your man a mighty warrior for His glory. Partner with the One who can do all things!

Love, Chris

An excellent wife is the crown of her husband,
but she who shames him is as rottenness in his bones.

PROVERBS 12:4

Her husband is known in the gates,
when he sits among the elders of the land.

PROVERBS 31:23

On Resolving Conflict

But let everyone be quick to hear,

slow to speak and slow to anger.

James 1:19

On Resolving Conflict

Dear Molly,

I realized very early in my marriage (around the second day) that Mac and I were two entirely different human beings with two entirely different thinking patterns. In my naivete, I thought that because we were now "one" there would never be any conflict of interests or ideas. (Goodness, what was I thinking?) A lesson I have learned over these years, however, is to both marvel and respect the way God has uniquely designed my husband; and believe me, he is quite unique (even though he is an identical twin)! I encourage you to also appreciate the way God has created your husband's heart and mind. Realize conflicts will come, because you are different. Two ways I have learned not to handle these situations are:

> **Don't be a pouter.** This is the approach my personality is most likely to take. I don't have to say anything; my lower lip says it all! Sometimes Mac has no idea I am even "punishing" him with this cold silent treatment, which of course makes me even more outdone. Trust me, pouting does not resolve anything. Your husband cannot read your mind; so speak it with gentleness and respect.

> **Don't be a shouter.** The opposite of the cold shoulder route is the hot temper approach. This plan of action, or I should say, this unplanned reaction, can spew damaging and unnecessary fire into a relationship. Know that harsh words cannot be retrieved from the recipient's heart. *Believe a gentle answer turns away wrath (Proverbs 15:1).*

So we can't pout and we can't shout; what then is a woman to do? My ongoing advice to myself and now to you, is threefold:

Pray. Before you speak to your man, speak to the Lord. Tell Him everything you feel about the particular situation between you and your husband. Pour out your heart before the Lord. He is full of understanding and mercy.

Gain perspective. Through prayer, God will help you to see the conflict through His eyes. Hear what He has to say through His Word and His Spirit. Be willing to be convicted if you are wrong or humble if you are right. And then, be willing to …

Seek peace. Always know the Lord will call you to put aside malice and put on love. He is the Author of peace, so through Him, you can resolve any conflict.

Remember you are one with your husband, created for the purpose of walking together through life peacefully. Do not let the Enemy break your strides. Because marriage is God's design, the Deceiver's task is to destroy it. I encourage you to fight the Enemy, not your husband.

Love, Chris

Seek peace, and pursue it.

PSALM 34:14

On Forgiveness

Be kind to one another, tenderhearted,
forgiving each other,
just as God in Christ also has forgiven you.

Ephesians 4:32

On Forgiveness

9

Dear Molly,

The word "forgiveness" is as challenging to me as the word "submit", is it not? I tend to cry from within, "What about me? What about my rights, my hurts?" The mysterious thing about forgiveness is this: when you lay down your rights and your hurts at the foot of the cross, you are set free from them. Forgive your husband, and free yourself.

Just as conflict is inevitable, forgiveness is a choice, and I encourage you to choose it. Resolve your conflicts, and then also let them go. *Love does not act unbecomingly, does not seek its own, is not provoked, does not take into account a wrong suffered (1 Corinthians 13:4-5).*

If this command is difficult for you (which it most likely will be), call on Christ in time of need; He knows how to forgive. What you cannot naturally do, He can supernaturally do through you. Trust Him, and He will be your help, your guide and, ultimately, your peace.

The alternate choice is unforgiveness; there is really not a third option. But if you take the unforgiving route, the divide between husband and wife only becomes deeper and wider. I have found that not only does unforgiveness interfere with Mac and me, but it also inhibits my relationship with the Lord. My communication line is temporarily disconnected with Him because of clouded feelings of anger, bitterness, and discontentment. So, I have both isolated myself from my soul mate on this earth, as well as drawn away from the One who loves my soul the most!

Forgive your husband the way Christ forgave you. Also, pray for him the way Christ prays for you. Pray his heart would be softened, and then convicted of any hurt he may have caused you. Humbled hearts of repentance and forgiveness will keep your marriage full of love and acceptance, even in the midst of failures and miscommunications.

Forgiveness is the harder choice in the beginning, but it is always the right choice for a peace-filled ending.

Love, Chris

Blessed are the merciful,
for they shall receive mercy.

MATTHEW 5:7

Laugh Often

There is an appointed time for everything.

There is a time ... to laugh.

Ecclesiastes 3:1,4

10

Laugh Often

Dear Molly,

I hope laughter will be beautiful music played throughout your marriage. Laughter's melody is catchy and light-hearted, causing the binding stresses of life to unwind and release from your shoulders. Your laughter together will become sweet harmony not only to you but also to all those who hear it. Laugh often *with* your husband, your "partner of music."

I also encourage you to laugh often *at* your husband, in an uplifting way, of course. Even if you have heard the same joke for fifteen years, still chuckle. (I chuckle in amazement that Mac is still telling these same jokes!) You are your husband's audience, so laugh. I am convinced this is one of the reasons Mac picked me to be his wife – my gullibility to fall for a joke, and my laughter at his jokes, was just what he needed to keep on performing. (God help me!) Remember, humor in a marriage brings harmony to the home.

And then, I encourage you to laugh at yourself. Laugh at the burnt chicken, (the burnt pizza, the burnt grilled cheese, the burnt green beans that are shellacked to the bottom of the pan). Laugh at locking your keys in your running vehicle that contains your groceries, purse, and phone.

Laugh at showing up for your child's friend's birthday party a week early or a week late. (I've done both.) Choose to laugh at your imperfections instead of sinking under them. Your mistakes do not define you. They may humble you a little bit, but Jesus Christ defines you…and Jesus is JOY…and joy from within becomes bubbling laughter.

Together, continually seek true joy in your marriage. As you do, others will want to join in with your sweet melodious tune.

Love, Chris

God has made laughter for me;
everyone who hears will laugh with me.

GENESIS 21:6

Our mouth was filled with laughter and our tongue with joyful singing . . .
"The Lord has done
great things for us; we are glad."

PSALM 126:2-3

Wife — Mother — Other

For this cause a man shall leave his father and mother
and cleave to his wife; and they shall become one flesh.

Genesis 2:24

Her children rise up and bless her;
her husband also ... praises her.

Proverbs 31:28

...and let her works praise her in the gates.

Proverbs 31:31

Wife – Mother – Other

Dear Molly,

I encourage you to always remember your God-given priorities as a married woman. You, from the day of your wedding ceremony, have the high privilege to be called *wife*. This is your first title, and always your first responsibility, before any other relationship. In God's eyes, this position is a high place of honor. The marriage relationship is meant to be a beautiful representation of God's commitment of everlasting love to His people. He desires your marriage to display this kind of sweet love. Realize your devotion to your husband will ultimately bring glory to the Lord. So keep your man the top priority – love him well, with the love of Christ.

Secondly, Lord willing, you will be given the title *mother*. With this role you will experience a broad spectrum of emotions – from inexplicable delight to absolute exasperation, from endless energy to sheer exhaustion, from sweet moments of bliss to enduring trials of toddlerhood. Mothering will take all of your day and many of your nights. How then do we keep "wife" as number one priority? Realize that keeping your husband first is not defined by amount of time spent in each role; it's a matter of the heart. Your *heart* needs to stay devoted to your husband even in the midst of the time-consuming care of your children. He needs to know where he stands with you, and so do your children, for that matter. I have read, and do believe it is true, a child will find a strong sense of self-security within their parents' love for each other. In this case, they are never forced to pick sides. Realize your husband, who will have earned the title *daddy*, will be one of your greatest assets in your mothering. Parenting is a partnership. I encourage you to lock arms with him and walk this road together prayerfully. Children are gifts from God … enjoy your gifts, created by your love, together.

The third priority is using any other unique God given gift or talent. Do not feel pressure to seek this *"other"* out, especially while the kids are young. God will let you know what and when and how to serve Him. For example, my "other" has ranged from coaching kids, to teaching women, to writing books. I have thoroughly enjoyed all these things and more. My goal however in the midst of my full schedule, is not to let these things become more important to me than my husband or my children. They do not need to receive my left over emotional and physical energy. The world will tell you just the opposite, the "other" is the more satisfying reward. But listen to the Lord. He says *an excellent wife is worth far above jewels (Proverbs 31:10).* Stay on the route of richness found in Him—*wife, mother, other.*

Love, Chris

A woman who fears the Lord, she shall be praised.

PROVERBS 31:30

A Healthy Hobby

And by the seventh day

God completed His work which He had done;

and He rested on the seventh day from all His work ...

Genesis 2:2

A Healthy Hobby

Dear Molly,

I encourage you to allow Ryan to freely pursue a healthy hobby. Over the years, I have discovered that Mac's temporary absence has brought him more energy when he is physically present. Ryan will appreciate you when he feels the freedom to go and enjoy something of his choosing.

I must admit, in the early years of marriage, this hobby idea was much more difficult then than it is today. There were times I had to force a friendly smile when he walked out the door to go play golf or go hunt. We learned together how to give to each other concerning our personal outings. Here are some guidelines to pray over this matter:

1. Pray his hobby would not become overly time-consuming. Discuss with your husband a reasonable amount of time to be away from you and the kids. This time will vary over the years. For example, Mac used to hunt alone, leaving all four young ones behind with me (these were my "forced-smile" years). But now, both boys can go enjoy with him. So, the amount of time away has lengthened; and instead of saying, "Hurry home," I say, "Take your time!"

2. Pray his hobby would bring him godly friends to keep him accountable throughout his life. I am humbly thankful for the incredible friends Mac

has gained through hangin' with his huntin' buddies. These friends speak truth into him, which is a blessing to me.

3. Pray his hobby would make him a better husband and a better daddy when he comes home. Pray that God would use this time to work in his heart – to refill and refresh him so he can get back in the game of life.

Now Molly, in the same way you are showing Ryan love by giving him time, I encourage you to also take time for yourself. You, too, need refreshment from the everyday-life routine. Do not disregard yourself in this way; it's easy to do, but no one benefits from this self-neglect.

Give time away; enjoy time away; and then, love time together.

Love, Chris

How precious is Your loving-kindness, O God!
And the children of men take refuge
in the shadow of Your wings.
They drink their fill of the abundance of Your house;
And You give them to drink the river of Your delights.

PSALM 36:7-8

Together Time

"How beautiful you are my darling,
how beautiful you are!"

Song of Solomon 1:15

"How handsome you are,
my beloved, and so pleasant!"

Song of Solomon 1:16

Together Time

Dear Molly,

As you continue in your marriage to Ryan, you will find that your lives together will fall into an everyday routine of life. For Ryan, his job will consist of daily stresses and pressures of work. For you, in your wife-mother-other roles, your to-do list will be ongoing and unending. To name a few: laundry will follow a flowing hill-mountain-hill pattern, while bills follow the incoming, outgoing, incoming, outgoing schedule; groceries will continue their disappearing act, while dust and clutter will steadily perform the opposite; the beds will be made and un-made for years to come, as well as the dishes – clean to unclean. Dare I even mention the out-of-the-home responsibilities of work and play? The ebb-and-flow-battle can be both exhausting and discouraging. Here is how I have learned to fight discouragement: accept and approach, then retreat and enjoy.

My biggest advice is to internally *accept.* Accept the truthful statement that "a woman's work is never done!" I think that is what God was trying to tell us in Proverbs 31. Through Christ's strength and perspective (which is the secret of Proverbs 31), you can then externally *approach* your job of "wife/mother/other-ing" with perseverance.

On the other hand, there is also a time to temporarily *retreat* from your labor. I encourage you to step out of the everyday routine of life and step into being a bride again. Keep dating your husband. When Mac takes me out, I put the laundry down, forget about the clutter, momentarily stop what's in front of me, and *enjoy*. My husband is a breath of fresh air to me. He makes me smile; he makes me chuckle; and yes, he makes me belly-laugh. But if I do not get away with him, sometimes his sense of humor isn't so funny. Instead, it can be quite irritating and untimely if you want the honest truth. Mac has figured out that all his flirtatious pinches,pokes, squeezes, and jabs need to be accompanied with quality time together, otherwise the outcome is not quite what he desired. When he takes me out, however, he can flirt all he wants! So take time away together to reconnect. This will help you come back with renewed strength and perspective to the mountain-hill-mountain phenomena going on in your laundry room.

Accept the high call of being a wife and all that it entails and approach it with the unending perseverance of Christ. Then, retreat on a timely basis with the love of your life and enjoy your breath of fresh air.

Love, Chris

Let your fountain be blessed, and
rejoice in the wife of your youth.

PSALM 34:14

Daddy, the Hero

Honor your father and your mother,
that your days may be prolonged
in the land which the Lord your God has given you.

Exodus 20:12

Daddy, the Hero

Dear Molly,

Over the years of your marriage, Lord willing, you will transition together into the awesome role of parenting. Each of you will possess a love for your children that is deep and pure and beautiful. This God-given love will enable you to both tend to the tangible challenges of physical care, as well as pursue the intangible responsibilities of developing the character of each child. One of your intangible responsibilities as Mommy is to make sure that Daddy is your child's greatest hero. Children will do this naturally; so really, your job is to maintain and encourage this endearing relationship.

It's important to know that your children's relationship to their Daddy will be a mirror image of your relationship with your husband. Always know that little eyes are watching, little ears are listening, and little hearts and minds are being molded daily. Children are excellent imitators; so, teach with your actions. For example:

If you show kindness to your husband, they learn kindness towards their daddy.

If you show respect towards him, they learn how to respect him, and others.

If you uplift and encourage, they will learn to do the same.

Be cautiously aware that the opposite is true:

If you are unkind to your husband, they will learn unkindness.

If you are disrespectful to your husband, they learn disrespect, not only towards their daddy, but also, towards other authority as well.

If your words tear down and discourage, these are the words your children hear and learn to mimic.

God has given you the awesome privilege of being your children's teacher. Teach them to live by the way they see you live, day in and day out. Love your husband, and they will love their daddy. Listen to your husband, and they will listen to their daddy. Honor your husband, and they will have a hero in their home.

Love, Chris

Therefore, be imitators of God,
as beloved children; and walk in love,
just as Christ also loved you,
and gave Himself up for us, an offering and
a sacrifice to God as a fragrant aroma.

EPHESIANS 5:1-2

Keep Growing

But his delight is in the law
of the Lord, and in His law
he meditates day and night.
And he will be like a tree
firmly planted by streams of water,
which yields its fruit in its season,
and its leaf does not wither;
and in whatever he does, he prospers.

Psalm 1:2-3

15

Keep Growing

Dear Molly,

I encourage you to grow continually in the knowledge and understanding of Jesus' love. As I have written in a previous letter, learning of His intimate love for my soul has been the basis of everything God has taught me concerning life and marriage. Without His love I was a disconnected branch, broken and unfruitful. But God, in His abounding grace, pursued me and has captured me with His love. Because of Him in me, I have a sweet peace that I cannot describe, an overwhelming joy that I cannot contain, and an eternal hope that carries me through each day. *When I found him whom my soul loves; I held on to him and would not let him go (Song of Solomon 3:4).*

I urge you to seek the love of Christ. Remember, He delights in you! You will find His love imprinted on His hands; you will find His love imprinted on the pages of Scripture; and then, your husband will find His love imprinted on your heart. Through the years, your husband will observe how you speak, how you give, how you serve … how you live. The gentle strength of your character has the ability to move him to become more like Christ. And as he resembles his Savior, you will both benefit. I pray you will continue to stay rooted and grounded in God's rich love so your marriage will blossom with a fragrant beauty.

Over these past fifteen years, I have watched God beautifully mold the heart of my husband. My love for Mac runs deep – deeper than the love I had for him when I said the words "I do" as a young twenty-two-year-old. We've walked life together. And I look forward to the years to come – more walking, and an even deeper love. No, he's not perfect, and I'm not perfect, which means we have an imperfect marriage. But, we both know and claim our perfect Savior in the midst of all of our imperfections. When we keep Christ's unfailing love as the tie that binds, we become more like the tree firmly planted by streams of water … growing and flourishing together.

Stay close to your Perfect Love … Jesus. He will groom and grow and bless your marriage. Then, in the years to come, look forward to an even deeper love for your man as you walk life together.

Love, Chris

Blessed is the man who trusts in the Lord

and whose trust is the Lord. For he will be like a tree planted by the water that extends its roots by a stream and will not fear when the heat comes. But its leaves will be green, and it will not be anxious in a year of drought nor cease to bear fruit.

JEREMIAH 17:7-8

10 Years Later...
10 More Lessons

Backwards, Forwards, and In Between

So teach us to number our days,

that we may present to You

a heart of wisdom.

Psalm 90:12

Backwards, Forwards, and In Between

Dear Molly,

Goodness, it's been a little more than 10 years since I wrote my letters to you when you were a new bride. In this passing decade, much has changed. You now have four young children of your own and my four kids have all grown up and gone to college and beyond. Crazy to think how time and events forge onward in a (sometimes long) blink of an eye!

Over these years of life with Mac and our growing kids, I have learned more lessons in marriage that I want to share with you. Again, these lessons have not dropped out of the sky with ease and grace; but rather, they have each been experienced through both the highs and lows of authentic relationship. As you know and have experienced by now, marriage is full of trial and error, perseverance and commitment, tears and joy. Truly, it's about saying "I do" over and over and over again.

In this letter, I want to encourage you to *look backward*. Take the time to ponder all that has happened in the first decade of your relationship. Thank the Lord for both the trials and the blessings that have molded your marriage into what it is today. Thank Him for His faithfulness.

Then take a moment to *look forward*. Lord willing, someday, you and Ryan will also be sending your four little ones out the door of your home to start their own adventures. I know this is hard to fathom right now, but it will be just the two of you once again. God has a plan for this stage of marriage too.

And now, Molly, *cherish the present*. Join together with Ryan and be filled with gratitude for the past and hope for the future. Daily, be on the same team, first as husband and wife, and then as parents. Remember, children are gifts to adore not idols to worship. Encourage each other to stay the course in this stage of your journey; walk hand-in-hand, filled up with His love.

Love, Chris

You have enclosed me behind and before,
and laid Your hand upon me.

PSALM 139:5

Interesting Order

But as the church is subject to Christ,

so also wives ought to be to their husbands in everything.

Husbands, love your wives…

Ephesians 5:24-25

Interesting Order

Dear Molly,

This letter is a review lesson about the dreaded "S" word: submit. I have to confess; this Biblical command really irritates me at times. Why do I have to be the one to submit? And if I do, how in the world is my voice going to be heard?

Well, the bottom line here is this: I must trust God's word. And trusting His word means obeying it, even when I don't want to. Interestingly, when looking at the marriage verses in the Bible, I notice that the Lord addresses the wife first, then the husband. So, in my mind, I understand that not only do I have to submit, I also have to "go first" in this relational interaction. Ugh! (Sometimes I like to say to myself, "I have to be the mature one first," and this strangely makes me feel better.)

The thing is, when I do choose to respect Mac, I then find out that this act gives him the opportunity to love me. Think of it this way, Mac cannot hold my hand if my fist is clinched with frustration, and he cannot kiss my lips if they're curled up in anger, nor would he want to! These kinds of emotions can be very real when difficult situations arise, and there may be much truth to them. However, I have learned that it's best to take my issues to the Lord first, and wrestle with Him in prayer. In this place, I remember two things: one, when I submit to my husband, I am really submitting to God's word; and two, God is able to overrule any man's decision. I must unswervingly trust Him (the Lord), and then sweetly respect him (my husband). In keeping this God-designed order, blessings will flow. I have been married for two and a half decades now, and I can tell you, obeying God's word works out way better than disobeying God's word. Trust God's word; obey God's word.

So, "go first". Kindly submit with a gentle and quiet spirit, praying effectively and fervently to your God all along the way, and see what happens next. Your husband just may reach out and hold your hand; and after that, he may lean in and kiss your lips.

Love, Chris

Wives be subject to your husbands
as fitting to the Lord;
husbands love your wives,
and do not be embittered against them.

COLOSSIANS 3:18-19

Extended Love

The lovingkindness of the Lord reaches to the heavens,
Your faithfulness reaches to the skies.

Psalm 36:5

Extended Love

Dear Molly,

By now you have had many years' worth of sharing your life with your extended family, both on your side and on Ryan's side. I know this outpouring of love can be complicated at times due to all kinds of personalities, expectations, and opinions that enter into the family mix.

My simple advice is to talk things through together with your husband and come up with healthy boundaries concerning your extended family. Personally, I have found that when the boundaries are respected, I have energy to engage fully and embrace eagerly. However, when these lines are crossed, both my energy level and heart attitude changes, and things begin to unravel. Healthy boundaries bring healthy blessings.

Also realize you hold the "relational thermometer" when it comes to all your extended family, especially your mother and father-in-law. Choose to keep your heart and home warm and inviting to them, as well as all of the brothers, sisters, nieces, and nephews that come through your door. Choose to be kind and intentional in ways that are fitting with each one. Most often, the requirement is simply sincere hugs and flowing conversations. If you have a long-distance relationship with your in-laws, texting or phone-calling can brighten their day, especially if they get to hear the sweet voices of their grandchildren. God loves family unity; ask Him to give you what you need to embrace His design. He is for you, and He will help you love your extended family.

Be wise with your boundaries; be intentional with your kindness; be blessed by extending your love.

Love, Chris

For this reason I bow my knees before the Father, from whom every family in heaven and on earth derives its name, that He would grant you, according to the riches of His glory, to be strengthened with power through the inner man, so that Christ may dwell in your hearts through faith; and that you, being rooted and grounded in love, may be able to comprehend with all the saints what is the breadth and length and height and depth, and to know the love of Christ which surpasses knowledge, that you may be filled up to all the fullness of God.

EPHESIANS 3:14-19

Remember, He's a Man

Then the Lord God formed man
of dust from the ground,
and breathed into his nostrils
the breath of life;
and man became a living being.

Genesis 2:7

Remember, He's a Man

Dear Molly,

Do you ever wonder what's going on in that husband's head of his? Or do you wonder why in the world he does what he does when he does it? (You don't have to answer these questions; I already know, and I get it!) I want to encourage you whenever you enter into this bewildered state:

1. Remember, he's a man, not a woman. In general, men think and act differently than women in almost every way; but somehow, I tend to forget this obvious truth. For example, when it comes to personal home décor, I have lovely pictures of painted songbirds in my dining room, but Mac has chosen other birds in his study that he himself has shot, stuffed, and mounted. Another example, when it comes to movies, most any chick flick will do for me; but for Mac, the more blood, guts, and battle scenes, the better. Men are warriors at heart, and really, that's a good thing. We are to encourage our men in their manliness and then watch them both fight for us and protect us.

2. Remember, he's a man, not Jesus. This is important. Do not expect your husband to do what only Jesus can do. Keep in mind, man was made from

dust; at best, he's a limited "earthling". But also remember who Jesus is: He created the dust, and He created your man. Your husband cannot read your mind, so speak your thoughts out loud, gently. And he cannot completely understand your heart, so give him grace. The beautiful truth is, Jesus *can* read your mind and He *does* understand your heart. Continually run to Him and He will help you with your man.

So when you and your husband don't see things from the same vantage point, learn to chuckle at the complexity of your dusty man. Then lean into your Perfect God-Man, Jesus, trusting that He will hear, understand, and meet your every need.

Love, Chris

Therefore, just as through one man sin entered the world...
much more did the grace of God and
the gift by the grace of the one Man,
Jesus Christ, abound to many.

ROMANS 5:12,15

Wise Counsel

Listen to counsel and accept discipline,

that you may be wise the rest of your days.

Proverbs 19:20

Wise Counsel

Dear Molly,

I'm pretty sure you will agree with this statement: with marriage comes conflict. These struggles may be over little things, or they may be over BIG things.

For the little things: I've learned to repeat this borrowed phrase often, "Keep the little things little." In other words, don't grow a petty argument or a differing opinion, and don't try to win a small battle just for the sake of winning. Let it go, embrace peace instead. Remember, both of you may be looking at a certain issue from two different sides, but this does not mean one of you is right and the other is wrong. Over the years, if a particular struggle between Mac and me continues, I have developed a "3-day-pray" rule. I simply make a choice to say very *little* to Mac about the situation, but for three days, I say *much* to the Lord about it in prayer. I ask the Lord to check my motives and to give me His heavenly perspective, not just my side-ways one. By the third day, interestingly and often, the little thing that was between us has either disappeared altogether, or we have come to a peaceful agreement over it.

For the BIG things: If you are unable to resolve an ongoing issue between yourselves, be willing to get wise Christian counseling. A third party, steeped in God's word and His wisdom will bring fresh insight and hopeful resolution. If you go this route, it is very important that you are certain your chosen counselor is getting all of his/her direction from the ultimate **Wise Counselor**. Pray that the Lord will show you the right person for your particular issue. There are many Spirit-led, trained, and experienced counselors, and there are many who are just the opposite. Use discernment.

When marriage brings conflict, let the conflict bring you to Jesus, so that Jesus can bring reconciliation, in both the little and the BIG things.

Love, Chris

But the wisdom from above is first pure, then peaceable, gentle, reasonable, full of mercy and good fruits, unwavering, without hypocrisy.
And the seed whose fruit is righteousness is sown in peace by those who make peace.

JAMES 3:17-18

Soften the Stiff Neck

A man who hardens his neck after much reproof will suddenly be broken beyond remedy.

Proverbs 29:1

Soften the Stiff Neck

Dear Molly,

Life gets so busy and full with raising a family that often the husband/wife role is usurped by the mommy/daddy role. Disciplining, meeting basic needs, as well as loving on your kids leaves you weary and exhausted. Then, when your husband walks through the door from a long day at work, what are you to do with this big guy of yours when he is added back into the family mix? The immediate and natural answer is to divide and conquer the parental responsibilities, which results in very little interaction between the two of you. Parental responsibilities, both in and out of the home, can take a toll on a marriage.

The Lord convicted me of this dilemma years ago, and from this place, I made a determined decision that I know has benefited our marriage for the long run. One thing I do to stay connected is this: before I go to bed each night, I choose to give Mac a neck massage as he sits in his recliner. And during this time, I silently pray for him (to lead his family well, to love God's word, to be a man of integrity, to understand me and his kids…). In those few short minutes, I believe the Lord reconnects us physically, emotionally, and spiritually. He is using my hands to "soften his stiff neck" in ways that I may not even be aware of, molding him through my requests. I know

God answers prayer, and through the years, Mac has willingly turned his head in the Lord's direction; and for that I am grateful.

I have to say, sometimes I am absolutely exhausted and there's nothing in me (except for Christ) that wants to give kindness in this way. And there are other times that I don't even think my husband deserves a neck massage, if you know what I mean. However, it's especially at this time, I choose to do it anyway. Softening the stiff neck goes both ways. I must soften my own attitude, and be the means of softening his. Be willing to touch your husband with your Christ-like molding, praying hands. It's a tough world out there. He needs your tender loving care, every day.

By the way, Mac's daily act of kindness for me is to make the coffee at night, so all I have to do in the morning is pour…ahh, bless him.

Love, Chris

Behold, like the clay in the potter's hand, so are you in My hand, O house of Israel.

JEREMIAH 18:6

Love in the Making

I am my beloved's, and his desire is for me.

Song of Solomon 7:10

Love in the Making

Dear Molly,

This lesson is rather uncomfortable for me because I'm somewhat of a private person about this topic, BUT I have to talk about sex in at least one of these letters. I mean, really, how does one write 25 years' worth of marriage lessons and NOT talk about sex?

So, with that being said, I'll be brief and to the point: sex is a physical need of your husband's, so give it to him. I know you are at an exhausting stage of your mothering right now; oh boy, how I remember! The last thing I wanted at the end of long draining day was THAT! But you must remember, sex is a need and you are the one (and only one) to fill it. Give him plenty of opportunity to *drink water from his own cistern (Proverbs 5:15).*

Here are a few tips that might help you in this area:

1. Earlier in the evening, tell yourself, "Tonight's the night." In doing so, you have time to mentally and emotionally prepare your physically tired body. (Mac has learned that taking me out on a date works wonders for me, and then…for him.)

2. On that night, do something to get yourself more in the mood—put on a little perfume, light a candle, wear something sexy, play some music, whatever helps you become a willing partner.

3. Be all there. This is not just about him; it's about you too. Sexual intercourse is not a "have-to practice of a disciplined wife". Lovemaking is the sweet and sacred act of husband and wife becoming one flesh all over again. When you give of yourself with this kind of heart and mind, body and soul, the end result is... satisfying, releasing, recommitting, reconnecting...beautiful.

Sex between husband and wife is God designed, God approved, and God blessed. It is the divine expression of holy matrimony. Indeed, it is love in the making.

Love, Chris

His mouth is full of sweetness. And he is wholly desirable.
This is my beloved and this is my friend.
SONG OF SOLOMON 5:16

Who he Is, not Who he Isn't

You formed my inward parts;

You weaved me

in my mother's womb.

Psalms 139:13

Who he Is, not Who he Isn't

Dear Molly,

Do you ever get frustrated with Ryan? (I'm grinning while writing this because I know, you know, that I know the answer.) I confess, there are times when I look at Mac and just shake my head in wonderment. I say to myself, "Why can't he be more *like this* or more *like that*?"

But then, I remember another lesson I have learned over the years. One day, in the midst of one of my bewildered states concerning my husband's personage, the Lord gently whispered to my heart, "Focus on who he is, not who he isn't?" This sounded simple enough, so I began to practice it. For example, Mac is a strong leader, full of passion in all he thinks, says, and does. However, because of this God-given trait of passion, he isn't as compassionate as I would like him to be at times. (In other words, he's not as compassionate as me. He should be more like me, right? Wrong.) My choice in this kind of personality assessment, is to either focus on who he is, respecting his abilities, or focus on who he isn't, insulting his character. Grace or judgment, acceptance or rejection, building up or tearing down; it's my choice. The wonderful thing that I have found is that when I support who he is, he does grow in both his strengths and his weaknesses. Thankfully, over our years together, Mac has gracefully given me room to grow up in my character, strengths and weaknesses, as well. When we give each other grace, we balance each other's character. He listens to me and I listen to him, and we operate together as one.

So compliment your husband in two ways. First, compliment him with kind words. Tell him who he is and why you love him. Secondly, compliment his personality with your personality. You are his counterpart, his coworker. Together you are one. You help him and he helps you. Live contentedly with who he is, not conflictingly with who he isn't.

Love, Chris

I will give thanks to you because I am fearfully and wonderfully made.

PSALMS 139:14

Decide Today, About Tomorrow

A wise woman builds her house.

Proverbs 14:1

Decide Today, About Tomorrow

Dear Molly,

I want to encourage you to view your marriage today as if you are in the process of building your "retirement home". Of course, the foundation of this house (marriage) is and can only be Christ Jesus. As I have mentioned in a previous letter, anything else is sinking sand.

Today, be intentional about the "bricks" you are adding to your foundation. These symbolic bricks can be brittle, full of unforgiveness and bitterness, or they can be solid, full of security and strength. Also, consider the "paint" on the walls of your home. Is it cold, dark, and uninviting, or light, warm, and welcoming? The analogy could go on and on. You have the awesome privilege of being both designer and decorator of your marital home both presently and in the future.

It's very important to realize that your attitude, your choice words, and your actions toward your husband today will determine what "home" you will live in many, many tomorrows from now. As you may know, building a real house is hard work with ups and downs throughout the entire process; well, so is marriage. Decide your choice "bricks" and lay them with steadfast love, then the end result is… gratification and contentment.

Here are three "building tips" for you to implement along the way:

Adore—Keep your love alive. Cherish your man *this* day.

Bless—Tell him often why you adore him. Speak love out loud.

Commit—Decide to stand by his side during this ongoing building process.

Invest now and you will not be sorry later. Your "retirement home" will be a welcoming place for you and your companion to live out your days in peace, security, and strength, as you walk together through both the highs and lows of life.

Love, Chris

Therefore everyone who hears these words of Mine and puts them into practice
is like a wise man who built his house on the rock. The rain came down,
the streams rose, and the winds blew and beat against that house; yet it did not fall,
because it had its foundation on the rock.
MATTHEW 7:24-25

Something New

Strength and dignity are her clothing,
and she smiles at the future.

Proverbs 31:25

Something New

Dear Molly,

At this moment, I know you can hardly envision your kids all grown up. But guess what? It happens! Before you know it, your little birds will start flapping their wings (brace yourself), and then, off they go, potentially in all different directions, leaving you and Ryan with an empty nest. When this day does finally come, you will want to both weep and rejoice at the same time. This change produces both an internal conflict and external adjustment that you will learn to embrace.

I encourage you to look forward to these years and this phase of your marriage. This past year was our first season of empty nesting. Mac and I transitioned from navigating-co-captains to nestled-in-companions. In this new phase of our lives, I decided that we needed to try new and different things together. Was Mac on board for this? Well, not really, but I told him we were much too young to become old fogies, so he relented. Our first new adventure was to take a series of dance lessons. Let me just say, there's nothing quite like learning to dance with four left feet and zero tempo between the two of us. With mutual agreement between us (as well as our dance instructor), we shuffled ourselves right out the dance studio door.

My point is, when you finally get to these years, be eager to experiment with new and different activities to do, trips to take, adventures to share. Make your husband your best friend in a whole new way. Remember though, as I mentioned to you in my previous letter, you are doing the relational-prep-work right now. Your future years depend on your present decisions. Before you know it, you will have your man all to yourself again (except for holidays and summers and weekend visits when the kids bring their friends along—some of your kids and others may even live with you again, but that's a lesson for another day.) Look forward to something new...with your aging man.

Embrace life every season ... *every day.*

Love, Chris

Behold, I will do something new,
now it will spring forth; will you not be aware of it?
I will even make a roadway in the wilderness, rivers in the desert.

ISAIAH 43:19

CHRIS BAXTER is a wife, mother, women's bible study teacher, writer, and speaker. She has been married to her husband, Mac, and together, they have four adult children: Maggie (married to AJ Gilmer), Brent, Davis, and Emmy. Some of Chris' writings include: *The Heartbeat of God, 25 Years/25 Lessons in Marriage, A Mother's Privilege,* and *Awesome Biblical Concepts: a Devotional for Every Family*; many of these books and devotionals can be found on her website at www.respitefortheweary.com. Her heart's desire is to be a "messenger of God's Word," whether in written or spoken form.

FOR MORE OF CHRIS BAXTER'S WRITING, CHECK OUT HER WEBSITE:

www.respitefortheweary.com

CPSIA information can be obtained
at www.ICGtesting.com
Printed in the USA
LVHW07*2135150418
573604LV00047B/552/P